W9-BNQ-446

EDMONTOSAURUS

Titles in the Dinosaur Profiles series include:

DINOSAUR PROFILES

EDMONTOSAURUS

Text by Fabio Marco Dalla Vecchia
Illustrations by Leonello Calvetti and Luca Massini

**BLACKBIRCH®
PRESS**

THOMSON

GALE

San Diego • Detroit • New ... Maine • London • Munich

Computer illustrations 3D and 2D: Leonello Calvetti and Luca Massini

Photographs: pages 22, 23 American Museum of Natural History, New York

LIBRARY OF CONGRESS CATALOGING-IN-PUBLICATION DATA

Dalla Vecchia, Fabio Marco.
 Edmontosaurus / text by Fabio Marco Dalla Vecchia; illustrations by Leonello Calvetti and Luca Massini.
     p. cm. — (Dinosaur profiles)
 Includes bibliographical references and index.
 ISBN 1-4103-0497-3 (paperback : alk. paper)
 ISBN 1-4103-0329-2 (hardback : alk. paper)
 1. Edmontosaurus—Juvenile literature. I. Calvetti, Leonello. II. Massini, Luca. III. Title.
IV. Series: Dalla Vecchia, Fabio Marco. Dinosaur profiles.

QE862.O65D35 2004
567.914—dc22   2004008697

Printed in China
10 9 8 7 6 5 4 3 2 1

Contents

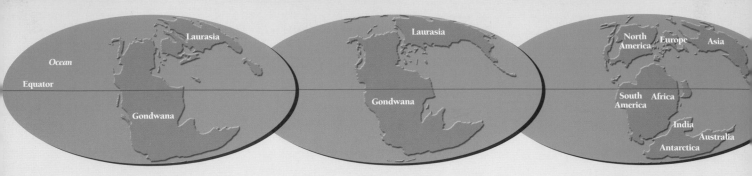

Late Triassic
227–206 million years ago

Early Jurassic
206–176 million years ago

Middle Jurassic
176–159 million years ago

A Changing World

Earth's long history began 4.6 billion years ago. Dinosaurs are some of the most fascinating animals from the planet's long past.

The word *dinosaur* comes from the word *dinosauria*. This word was invented by the English scientist Richard Owen in 1842. It comes from two Greek words, *deinos* and *sauros*. Together, these words mean "terrifying lizards."

The dinosaur era, also called the Mesozoic era, lasted from 248 million years ago to 65 million years ago. It is divided into three periods. The first, the Triassic period, lasted 42 million years. The second, the Jurassic period, lasted 61 million years. The third, the Cretaceous period, lasted 79 million years. Dinosaurs ruled the world for a huge time span of 160 million years.

Like dinosaurs, mammals appeared at the end of the Triassic period. During the time of dinosaurs, mammals were small animals the size of a mouse. Only after dinosaurs became extinct did mammals develop into the many forms that exist today. Humans never met Mesozoic

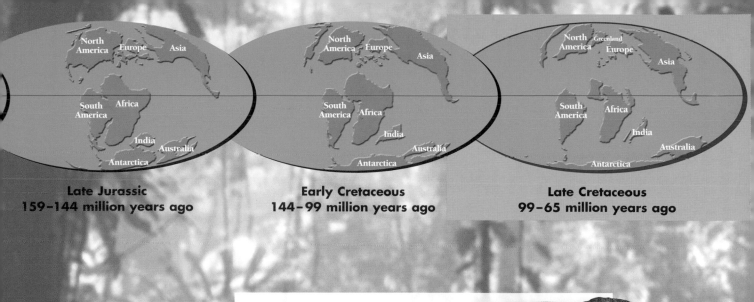

Late Jurassic
159–144 million years ago

Early Cretaceous
144–99 million years ago

Late Cretaceous
99–65 million years ago

dinosaurs. The dinosaurs were gone nearly 65 million years before humans appeared on Earth.

Dinosaurs changed in time. *Stegosaurus* and *Brachiosaurus* no longer existed when *Tyrannosaurus* and *Triceratops* appeared 75 million years later.

The dinosaur world was different from today's world. The climate was warmer, with few extremes. The position of the continents was different. Plants were constantly changing, and grass did not even exist.

A DUCKBILL

Edmontosaurus belongs to the group hadrosauria, or hadrosaurians. Hadrosaurians are called "duck-billed dinosaurs" or "duckbills" because of the shape of their snouts. Some hadrosaurians, like *Edmontosaurus*, were flat-headed. Others had unusual crests on their skulls. Paleontologists (scientists who study dinosaur fossils) are not sure what these crests were for. The crests might have been different in males and females or among animals in different species. Since the crests were hollow, they may have been used like a trumpet to make calling sounds.

An adult *Edmontosaurus* could be more than 33 feet (10 m) long and 6 feet (1.8 m) high at the hip. Its weight is estimated at between 2.3 and 3.1 tons (2.1 and 2.8 metric tons). It had no built-in defenses. But its large size and the fact that it lived in large herds protected it from most predators.

Edmontosaurus was bipedal, meaning it often moved on its hind feet. To do so, it lifted its tail from the ground and balanced it with the weight of its head and neck. It could also move on all fours. It was not a good runner, though. At the end of each front foot, *Edmontosaurus* had three main fingers that were webbed like a duck's feet. The fourth finger, similar to a human's little finger, was separate.

Edmontosaurus was among the last dinosaurs to exist on Earth. It lived 70 to 65 million years ago at the end of the Cretaceous period. The edmontosaurs lived in North America. At that time, a sea divided the continent in two,

A man could easily be crushed by an adult *Edmontosaurus*.

from the Gulf of Mexico to the north of Canada. *Edmontosaurus* remains have been found from Colorado to Saskatchewan. The duck-billed dinosaurs were the most common dinosaurs in North America, Asia, and Europe at the end of the Cretaceous period.

NORTH

AMERICA

Three *Edmontosaurus* species are known: *Edmontosaurus regalis*, *Edmontosaurus annectens*, and *Edmontosaurus saskatchewanensis*.

This map shows North America as it was in the Late Cretaceous period. The dark brown areas indicate mountains. The red dots indicate *Edmontosaurus* fossil discovery sites.

EDMONTOSAURUS BABIES

Young edmontosaurs had short snouts and large eyes. They hatched from large eggs about 8 inches (20 cm) long. The eggs were laid vertically in the bottom of a bowl-shaped nest. Nests were dug in the mud in open areas, such as islands in the middle of lakes. *Edmontosaurus* nested in colonies. All the females of the herd dug their nests in the same area, a few feet apart. In that way, the adults could better defend eggs and hatchlings from predators. *Troodon*, a small carnivorous (meat-eating) dinosaur, often roamed around the nesting areas waiting for a chance to snatch some of the eggs or hatchlings.

LIFE LESSONS

A newly hatched edmontosaur stayed in the nest and
was fed by its parents. After a while, the young edmontosaur had to learn
how to get its own food. Edmontosaurs ate only plants. A young edmontosaur
was too little to reach the leaves of trees. So its first meal was usually low-lying plants
in forest undergrowth or along stream banks. The young followed their parents in their
first exploration of the surrounding world, searching for food.

T.Rex Attack

Edmontosaurus lived in a land inhabited mainly by plant-eating dinosaurs. Small bipedal predators such as *Troodon* and *Dromaeosaurus* were no longer than 6.5 feet (2 m) long, including a long tail. They probably attacked only the young or the eggs. They were little threat to a herd of adult edmontosaurs. The biggest danger for the duck-billed dinosaurs was large predators such as *Tyrannosaurus Rex* or its close relative *Albertosaurus*. These fierce meat eaters usually attacked young, small, old, or sick dinosaurs, which were easier to kill.

Looking for Food

Edmontosaurus fed on plants that it grasped with its flat, wide snout. It ate the needles and branches of cone-bearing trees, seeds, and parts of other plants. The edmontosaur herds moved through forests searching for food. They ate an enormous amount of vegetation. When a herd passed through, a forest was nearly destroyed. But attacks by meat-eating dinosaurs prevented the plant-eating dinosaurs from becoming so numerous that they completely wiped out all the forest's vegetation.

THE EDMONTOSAURUS BODY

Edmontosaurus had strong jaws with powerful teeth perfect for grinding the tough plant materials that it ate. Its teeth were diamond shaped and small, but numerous. The teeth were arranged in layers, so that when a row of teeth was worn, it was soon replaced by a new row.

The tail was flat. It contained a network of thin bony rods that made it stiff and allowed it to be lifted from the ground when the animal moved. No fossil tracks of hadrosaurs have ever shown traces of tail dragging.

The back foot had three toes with rounded tips. Meat-eating dinosaurs had sharp claws, but edmontosaurs had flat, hooflike nails.

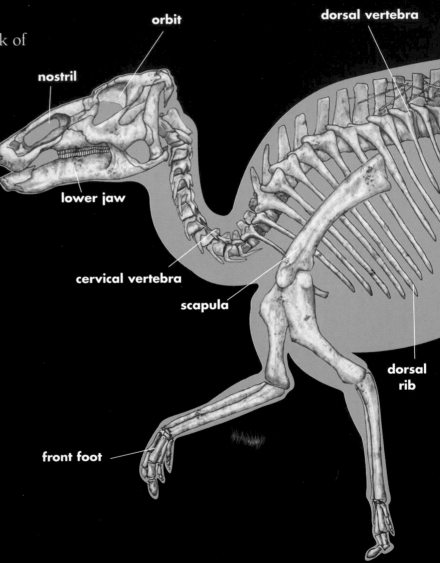

orbit

dorsal vertebra

nostril

lower jaw

cervical vertebra

scapula

dorsal rib

front foot

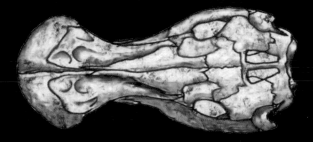

Dorsal view of skull. The expanded muzzle resembles that of a duck.

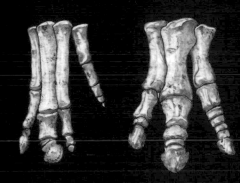

Left front foot   **Left back foot**

The ungual phalanges are heart shaped and flat.

caudal vertebra

bony rods

femur

tibia

tibia

fibula

back foot

19

Digging Up Edmontosaurus

The first skeleton of *Edmontosaurus* was discovered in Montana in 1891 by paleontologist John Bell Hatcher. The name *Edmontosaurus* (meaning "lizard of Edmonton") was invented by the paleontologist Lawrence Lambe in 1917. The name honored the town of Edmonton in Alberta, Canada. Complete skeletons of this dinosaur have been unearthed there.

In 1908, George Sternberg made an exciting discovery in Wyoming. He found an *Edmontosaurus* "mummy," a skeleton still covered by its petrified skin. The fossil is now exhibited at the American Museum of Natural History in New York City. Two years later, a second "mummy" was found. It is now exhibited at the Senckenberg Museum of Frankfurt am Main in Germany. The dead body was probably mummified by baking and drying under the sun. Then it was transported by water and covered with sand at the bottom of a river or a lake. The "mummy" of Frankfurt am Main even contains the fossilized remains of the dinosaur's last meal.

The number of fossil remains that have been found show that *Edmontosaurus* was very common along the coastal plains of North America. It is one of the few dinosaurs known from many complete or nearly complete skeletons.

Left: A mummified *Edmontosaurus* with preserved skin was found in 1908 by George Sternberg.

Below: The "mummy" is on display at the American Museum of Natural History in New York.

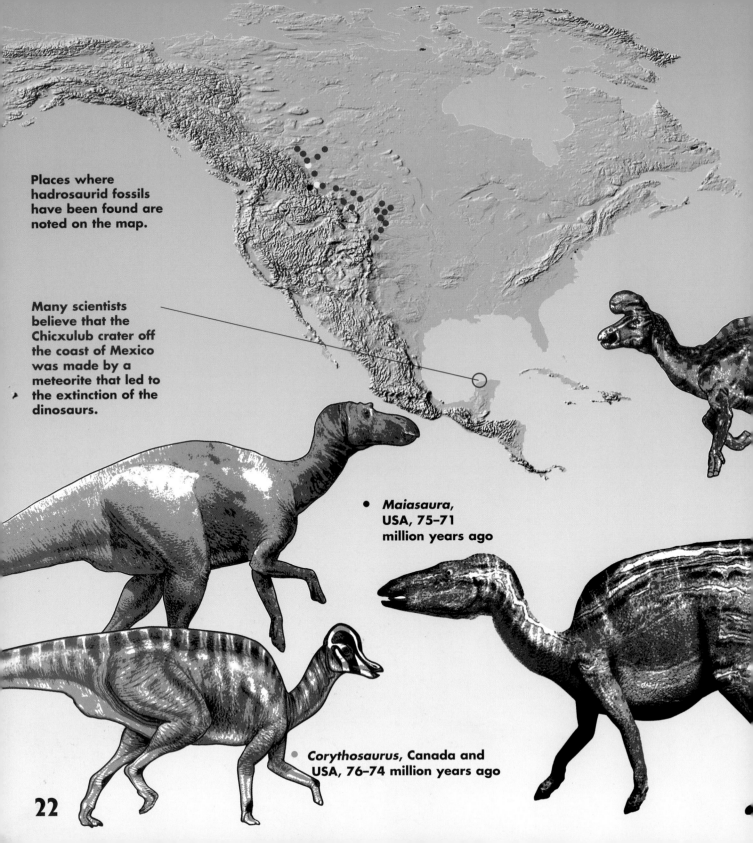

Places where hadrosaurid fossils have been found are noted on the map.

Many scientists believe that the Chicxulub crater off the coast of Mexico was made by a meteorite that led to the extinction of the dinosaurs.

Maiasaura, USA, 75–71 million years ago

Corythosaurus, Canada and USA, 76–74 million years ago

Lambeosaurus and **Corythosaurus** were crested hadrosaurids, while **Maiasaura** and **Edmontosaurus** were flat headed.

THE HADROSAURIDS

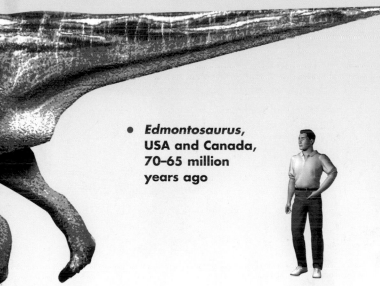

- **Lambeosaurus,** Canada and USA, 78–74 million years ago

- **Edmontosaurus,** USA and Canada, 70–65 million years ago

THE GREAT EXTINCTION

Sixty-five million years ago, when *Edmontosaurus* was one of the most common large animals on land, dinosaurs became extinct. This may have happened because a large meteorite struck Earth. A wide crater caused by a meteorite exactly 65 million years ago has been located along the coast of the Yucatán Peninsula in Mexico. The impact of the meteorite would have produced an enormous amount of dust. This dust would have stayed suspended in the atmosphere and blocked sunlight for a long time. A lack of sunlight would have caused a drastic drop of the earth's temperature and killed plants. The plant-eating dinosaurs would have died, starved and frozen. As a result, meat-eating dinosaurs would have had no prey and would also have starved.

Some scientists believe dinosaurs did not die out completely. They think that birds were feathered dinosaurs that survived the great extinction. That would make the present-day chicken and all of its feathered relatives descendants of the large dinosaurs.

THE EVOLUTION OF DINOSAURS

The oldest dinosaur fossils are 220–225 million years old and have been found mainly in South America. They have also been found in Africa, India, and North America. Dinosaurs probably evolved from small and nimble bipedal reptiles like the Triassic *Lagosuchus* of Argentina. Dinosaurs were able to rule the world because their legs were held directly under the body, like those of modern mammals. This made them faster and less clumsy than other reptiles.

Since 1887, dinosaurs have been divided into two groups based on the structure of their hips. Saurischian dinosaurs had hips shaped like those of modern lizards. Ornithischian dinosaurs had hips shaped like those of modern birds.

Triceratops is one of the Ornithischian dinosaurs, whose hip bones (inset) are shaped like those of modern birds.

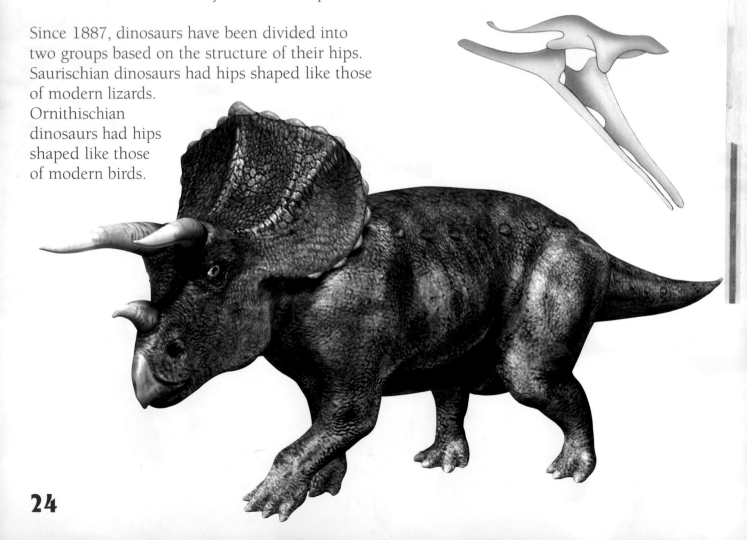

Tyrannosaurus is in the Saurischian group of dinosaurs, whose hip bones (inset) are shaped like those of modern lizards.

There are two main groups of saurischians. One group is sauropodomorphs. This group includes sauropods, such as *Brachiosaurus*. Sauropods ate plants and were quadrupedal, meaning they walked on four legs. The other group of saurischians, theropods, includes bipedal meat-eating predators. Some paleontologists believe birds are a branch of theropod dinosaurs.

Ornithischians are all plant eaters. They are divided into three groups. Thyreophorans include the quadrupedal stegosaurians, including *Stegosaurus*, and ankylosaurians, including *Ankylosaurus*. The other two groups are ornithopods, which includes *Edmontosaurus* and marginocephalians.

A DINOSAUR'S FAMILY TREE

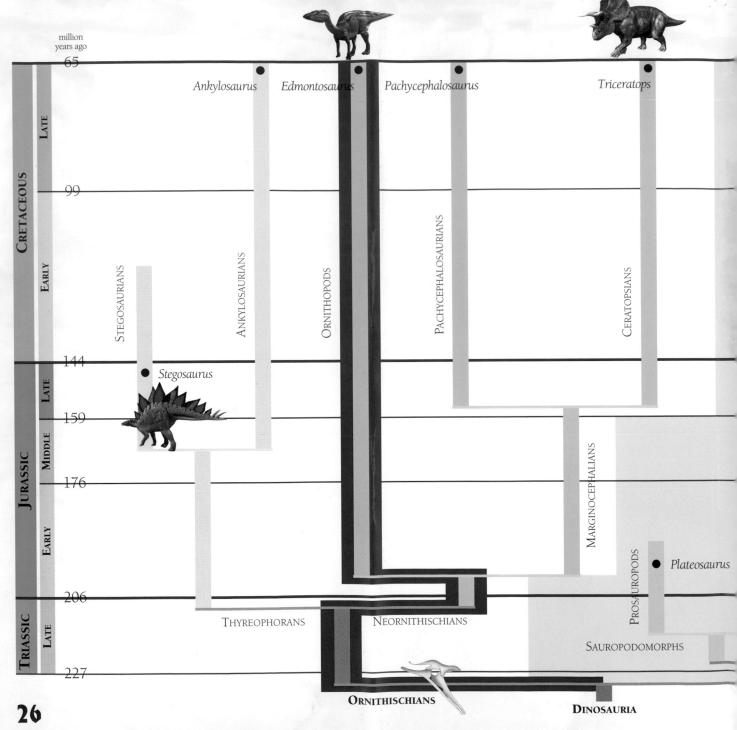

million years ago

65

CRETACEOUS

LATE

Ankylosaurus   Edmontosaurus   Pachycephalosaurus   Triceratops

99

EARLY

STEGOSAURIANS   ANKYLOSAURIANS   ORNITHOPODS   PACHYCEPHALOSAURIANS   CERATOPSIANS

144

Stegosaurus

LATE

159

JURASSIC

MIDDLE

176

MARGINOCEPHALIANS

EARLY

PROSAUROPODS   Plateosaurus

206

THYREOPHORANS   NEORNITHISCHIANS

TRIASSIC

LATE

SAUROPODOMORPHS

227

ORNITHISCHIANS   DINOSAURIA

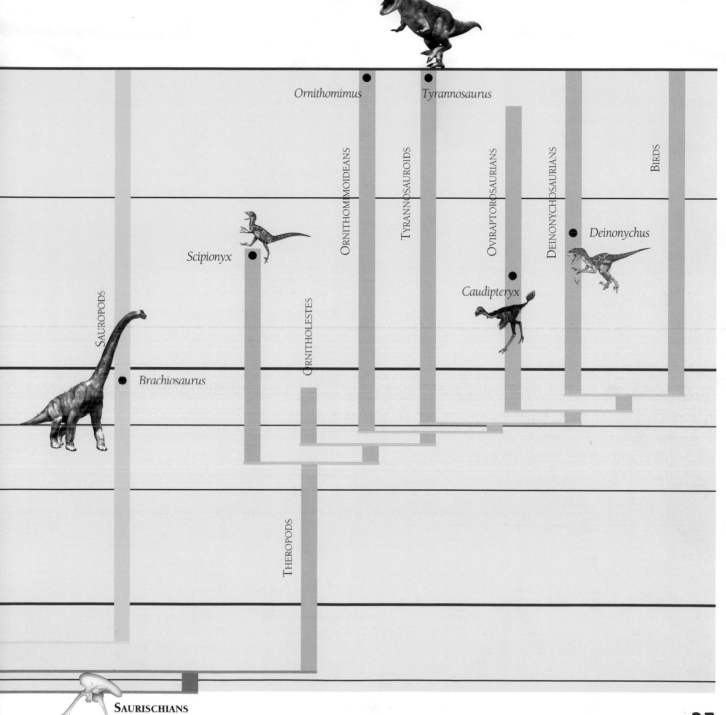

Ornithomimus

Tyrannosaurus

ORNITHOMIMOIDEANS

TYRANNOSAUROIDS

OVIRAPTOROSAURIANS

DEINONYCHOSAURIANS

BIRDS

Scipionyx

Deinonychus

Caudipteryx

SAUROPODS

ORNITHOLESTES

Brachiosaurus

THEROPODS

SAURISCHIANS

27

Glossary

Bipedal moving on two feet

Caudal related to the tail

Cervical related to the neck

Cretaceous Period the period of geological time between 144 and 65 million years ago

Dorsal related to the trunk

Egg a large cell enclosed in a shell produced by reptiles and birds to reproduce themselves

Femur thigh bone

Fibula the outer of the two bones in the lower leg

Fossil a part of an organism of an earlier geologic age, such as a skeleton or leaf imprint, that has been preserved in the earth's crust

Jurassic Period the period of geological time between 206 and 144 million years ago

Mesozoic Era the period of geological time between 248 and 65 million years ago

Meteorite a piece of iron or rock that falls to Earth from space

Orbit opening in the skull surrounding the eye

Paleontologist a scientist who studies prehistoric life

Quadruped an animal that moves on four feet

Scapula shoulder blade

Skeleton the structure of an animal body, made up of bones

Skin the outer covering of the animal body

Skull the bones that form the cranium and the face

Tibia shinbone

Triassic Period the period of geological time between 248 and 206 million years ago

Vertebrae the bones of the backbone

FOR MORE INFORMATION

Books

Paul M. Barrett, *National Geographic Dinosaurs.*
Washington, DC: National Geographic Society, 2001.

Tim Haines, *Walking with Dinosaurs: A Natural History.*
New York: Dorling Kindersley, 2000.

David Lambert, Darren Naish, and Elizabeth Wyse,
*Dinosaur Encyclopedia: From Dinosaurs to the Dawn of
Man.* New York: Dorling Kindersley, 2001.

Web Sites

The Cyberspace Museum of Natural History
www.cyberspacemuseum.com/dinohall.html
An online dinosaur museum that includes descriptions and illustrations.

Dinodata
www.dinodata.net
A site that includes detailed descriptions of fossils,
illustrations, and news about dinosaur research and
recent discoveries.

The Smithsonian National Museum of Natural
History
www.nmnh.si.edu/paleo/dino
A virtual tour of the Smithsonian's National Museum
of Natural History dinosaur exhibits.

About the Author

Fabio Marco Dalla Vecchia is the curator of the Paleontological Museum of Monfalcone in Gorizia, Italy. He has participated in several paleontological field works in Italy and other countries and has directed paleontological excavations in Italy. He is the author of more than fifty scientific articles that have been published in national and international journals.

INDEX

INDEX